Refactoring TypeScript

Keeping your code healthy

James Hickey

Refactoring TypeScript

Copyright © 2019 Packt Publishing

Author: James Hickey

Managing Editor: Aritro Ghosh

Acquisitions Editor: Karan Wadekar

Production Editor: Salma Patel

Editorial Board: Shubhopriya Banerjee, Bharat Botle, Ewan Buckingham, Megan Carlisle, Simon Cox, Mahesh Dhyani, Manasa Kumar, Alex Mazonowicz, Dominic Pereira, Shiny Poojary, Abhishek Rane, Erol Staveley, Ankita Thakur, and Jonathan Wray

First Published: October 2019

Production Reference: 1181019

ISBN: 978-1-83921-804-0

Published by Packt Publishing Ltd.

Livery Place, 35 Livery Street

Birmingham B3 2PB, UK

Table of Contents

Chapter 4: Nested Conditionals   *33*

Chapter 5: Primitive Overuse   *41*

Chapter 6: Lengthy Method Signatures 55

Chapter 7: Methods That Never End 65

Chapter 10: Conclusion

Preface

About the Book

Refactoring improves your code without changing its behavior. With refactoring, the best approach is to apply small targeted changes to a codebase. Instead of implementing a huge sweeping change to your code, refactoring is better as a long-term and continuous enterprise. *Refactoring TypeScript* explains how to spot bugs and remove them from your code.

You'll start by seeing how wordy conditionals, methods, and null checks make code unhealthy and unstable. Whether it is identifying messy nested conditionals or removing unnecessary methods, this book will show you various techniques to avoid these pitfalls and write code that is easier to understand, maintain, and test.

By the end of the book, you'll have learned some of the main causes of unhealthy code, tips to identify them and techniques to address them.

About the Author

With a background in creative arts, philosophy, and software development, **James Hickey** has been helping developers become software artisans and navigate their careers. He has worked professionally in web and mobile-based projects mentoring development teams and leading business-critical projects. His technical interests focus on software design and architecture.

Learning Objectives

- Spot and fix common code smells to create code that is easier to read and understand
- Discover ways to identify long methods and refactor them
- Create objects that keep your code flexible, maintainable, and testable
- Apply the Single Responsibility Principle to develop less-coupled code
- Discover how to combine different refactoring techniques
- Learn ways to solve the issues caused by overusing primitives

Audience

This book is designed for programmers who are looking to explore various refactoring techniques to develop healthy and maintainable code. Some experience in JavaScript and TypeScript can help you easily grasp the concepts explained in this book.

Approach

Each section in this book represents a 'code smell'. A code smell is an indication that a part of your code is rotting and becoming unhealthy. The first chapter of each section will introduce how to identify a specific code smell and why it is considered unhealthy. Then, you'll learn techniques that can be used to address the code issue - once you've explored the problem.

1

Introduction

About TypeScript

What Is It?

TypeScript (https://www.typescriptlang.org/) is a superset of JavaScript. That is, it's JavaScript with a bunch of additional features. After you've written your code, it compiles into JavaScript.

TypeScript was created by Microsoft and led by Anders Hejlsberg (who was one of the core members of the group that formed the C# programming language, among others).

TypeScript's primary features and benefits include the following:

- A fairly advanced type system
- Support for future and bleeding-edge JavaScript features
- Fantastic support for developer tooling inside IDEs

What's All the Fuss About?

TypeScript has gained a lot of traction in the past few years. In the 2019 Stack Overflow Developer Survey, TypeScript was rated as the #3 top-loved programming language (https://insights.stackoverflow.com/survey/2019#most-loved-dreaded-and-wanted)!

Why do developers love it so much?

From my own experience, it's because JavaScript (due to its dynamic nature) allows for some strange kinds of code. Also, because it's compiled at runtime, most bugs are discovered at runtime (in certain production scenarios, this can be too late to catch bugs!).

With TypeScript, on the other hand, you can define solid contracts by using types (classes, interfaces, types, implicit method return types, and so on). This enables the IDE you are using to immediately detect certain kinds of bugs as you type your code! It also makes your code more predictable and less error-prone since you have guaranteed method return types, for example.

> **Note**
>
> I remember the first time that I introduced TypeScript into a real-world project – it increased my productivity tons! I discovered bugs that I had no idea existed, either.

TypeScript versus JavaScript

I'd like to make a quick comparison between some vanilla JavaScript and TypeScript to give you an idea of what I've been talking about.

Let's take some valid code in JavaScript:

```
const myData = getMyData();
```

How do I know what the `getMyData` method will return? Will it return an object? A Boolean?

If it does return an object, how can I find out what the properties of the object are?

Other than digging into the source code for that method, I can't.

Inside that method, we could even do something strange, like this:

```
function getMyData(kind) {
    if(!kind)
        return false;
    else
        return { data: "hi" };
}
```

So... sometimes, this function returns a Boolean and other times it returns an object?

I've seen code like this in real-world production code bases. And yes – it's very hard to understand, debug, and test and is very prone to errors.

Using TypeScript, you can *lock down* the return type explicitly:

```
function getMyData(kind) : object {
    if(!kind)
        return false;
    else
        return { data: "hi" };
}
```

This would *not* compile since the method signature says that the method should always return an object, but the code can return a Boolean and an object.

Let's look at another example:

```
const user = {
    emailAddress: "test@test.com"
};

emailUser(user.emailAddress);

user.emailAddress = 2;

emailUser(user.emailAddress);
```

The second time we call **emailUser**, we are passing it a number instead of a string. That's what I mean by *strange code*.

In TypeScript, this would throw an error at compilation time (and in your IDE as you type).

You would find this issue immediately as you type. However, in JavaScript, you wouldn't know about this until you tried to send an email to a user at runtime.

What if this bug ended up only happening in certain production scenarios? In this case, by using TypeScript, you could avoid this error before you even commit the code in the first place!

Why I Chose TypeScript for This Book

I chose TypeScript as the language to use for this book because it has much in common with dynamic languages such as JavaScript, yet it also has common features from object-oriented type-safe languages such as Java and C#.

It has a good blend of object-oriented tools, functional tools, and the ability to still harness the dynamic nature of JavaScript if needed.

Most of the techniques in this book are generic and can be applied to most other programming languages. TypeScript just happens to be a good middle ground to use to showcase these problems and solutions!

What Is Refactoring?

Let's Define It

Refactoring is just a fancy term that means improving your code without changing how it behaves.

If improving the quality of your code introduces more bugs or changes how the system worked before, then is it really *improving* your code? Nope!

With refactoring, the best approach is to apply small targeted changes to a code base. Instead of making a huge sweeping change to your code, refactoring is better as a long-term, continuous enterprise.

Why? Applying larger changes all at once presents *more risk* and *more time* to implement.

We don't want that.

We want to improve the health of our code while maintaining control of our code/ software.

> **Note**
>
> It's important to have your code under test (unit, integration, and so on) as this will give you a safety net to ensure any code changes won't also change its behavior and cause bugs.
>
> While we won't look at building tests in this book, it's important to remember the importance of having tests.

Our Approach

I've found that many refactoring resources are hard to follow and easily overwhelming. They also tend to start at the wrong end by telling you what a pattern is before explaining what problem it solves.

Each category/section in this book represents some kind of *code smell*. A code smell is some indication that a part of your code is rotting and becoming unhealthy.

The first section of each category will introduce how to identify a specific code smell and why it is considered unhealthy. Then, we'll look at techniques that can be used to address the code issue – after we've explored the problem first!

Design Patterns

When learning about design patterns (https://en.wikipedia.org/wiki/Software_design_pattern), it's important to realize that these patterns are a form of refactoring tool.

Design patterns are meant to address issues around the fact that your code is not flexible enough, hard to maintain, and so on.

As you move through this book, the emphasis will be on looking at and solving specific code issues. Some of those issues just happen to be solvable using design patterns!

Why Refactor at All?

Slow Development

Ever work in a software system where your business asked you to build a new feature but once you started digging into the existing code, you discovered that it wasn't going to be so easy to implement?

Often, this is because our existing code is not flexible enough to handle the new behaviors the business wants to include in your application.

Why?

Well, sometimes, we take shortcuts and hack stuff in.

Perhaps we don't have the knowledge and skills to know how to write healthy code (this book will help!).

Other times, timelines need to be met at the cost of introducing these shortcuts.

This is why refactoring is so important:

Refactoring can help your currently restrictive code become flexible and easy to extend once again.

Code is like a living organism (https://meltingasphalt.com/a-codebase-is-an-organism/) – like a garden. Sometimes, you just need to get rid of the weeds!

> **Note**
>
> I've been involved in a software project where adding a checkbox to a screen was not possible given the system's setup at the time! Adding a button to a screen took days to figure out! And this was as a senior developer with a good number of years under my belt. Sadly, some systems are just very convoluted and hacked together.
>
> This is what happens when we don't keep our code healthy!

Saving Money

It's a practical reality that you need to meet deadlines and get a functioning product out to customers. This could mean having to take shortcuts from time to time, depending on the context. Bringing value to your customers is what makes money for your company, after all.

In the long term, however, these *quick-fixes* or shortcuts lead to code that can be rigid, hard to understand, more prone to contain bugs, and so on.

Improving and keeping code quality high leads to the following:

- Fewer bugs
- The ability to add new features faster
- The ability to keep changes to existing code isolated
- Code that's easier to reason about

All of these benefits lead to less time spent on debugging, fixing problems, developers trying to understand how the code works, and so on.

It saves your company real money!

Navy SEALS Get It

There's an adage that comes from the Navy SEALs that many have noticed also applies to the creation of software:

Slow is smooth. Smooth is fast.

Taking time to build quality code upfront will help your company move faster in the long term. But even then, we don't anticipate all future changes that need to be made to the code and still need to refactor from time to time.

Being a Craftsman

Software development is a critical part of our society.

Developers build code that controls the following:

- Vehicles
- Power grids
- Government secrets
- Home security
- Weapons
- Bank accounts
- And more!

I'm sure you can think of more cases where the software a developer creates is tied to the security and well-being of an individual or group of people.

Would you expect your doctor to haphazardly prescribe you medication without them carefully ensuring that they know what your medical condition is?

Wouldn't you want to have a vehicle mechanic who takes the time to ensure your vehicle's tires won't fall off while you are driving?

Being a craftsman is just another way of saying that we should be professional and care about our craft.

We should value quality software that will work as intended!

I've had it happen before that my car's axel was replaced and, while I was driving away, the new axel fell right out of my car! Is that the kind of mechanic I can trust my business with? Nope!

Likewise, the quality of software that we build can directly impact people's lives in real ways.

Case Study #1

You might be familiar with an incident from 2018 where a Boeing 737 crashed and killed all people on board. It was found that Boeing had outsourced its software development to developers who were not experienced in this particular industry. Also, these developers were having to redo improperly written code over and over again.

It is clear from this example how it can be inefficient and even dangerous when a group of developers are lacking the knowledge or tools to build quality software in such critical systems.

For Boeing in general, what did this overall lack of quality and craftsmanship lead to?

The company's stocks took a huge dip a couple of days after the crash.

Oh, and don't forget – people died. No one can undo or fix this.

After this was all said and done, Boeing did not benefit from cutting costs, trying to rush their software development, and focusing on speed rather than quality.

As software development professionals, we should seek to do our part and value being software craftsmen and craftswomen who focus on creating quality software.

> **Note**
>
> You can find the full article here: https://www.bloomberg.com/news/articles/2019-06-28/boeing-s-737-max-software-outsourced-to-9-an-hour-engineers.

Case Study #2

Do you still think that because airplanes can potentially kill people that the software that's built is going to be quality? Nope.

Here's another example of software quality issues in the aviation field: a $300 million Airbus software bug solved by turning it off and on again every 149 hours (https://gizmodo.com/turn-it-off-and-on-again-every-149-hours-is-a-concernin-1836818094).

Sounds kind of like a memory leak, right? You know, when you have a web application that starts getting slow and clunky after keeping it open for a while? Just refresh the page and voila! Everything's fine again!

Sadly, we are building airplanes like that too.

Quoting the article:

"Airlines who haven't performed a recent software update on certain models of the Airbus A350 are being told they must completely power cycle the aircraft every 149 hours or risk "...partial or total loss of some avionics systems or functions," according to the EASA."

Do you want to fly on those planes?

Quality matters. And the fact is, many developers are *not* writing quality software.

I hope that this book will help developers get just a *little bit better* at building quality software.

When Should I Refactor?

It's already been mentioned that refactoring is best done in smaller chunks rather than in big sweeping changes.

Again, this avoids riskier and error-prone changes. You can also ship your product to your customers in a more iterative way and get feedback from your users earlier.

Then, the question arises: *When should I refactor?*

The Boy Scout Rule

There's a programming principle called *The Boy Scout Rule* (http://www.informit.com/articles/article.aspx?p=1235624&seqNum=6) which states:

"Leave the code cleaner than you found it."

This applies whether you are fixing a bug, adding a new feature, and so on. Just do something that improves the code you are working with.

> **Note**
>
> It could be as simple as adjusting the name of an ambiguous variable name.
>
> It could be reorganizing the structure of your code's files.
>
> It could be introducing design patterns to solve specific issues.

Repetitive Work

Ever run into a situation where you need to write code that you've already written before? Maybe the same code already exists somewhere else in the system?

If you find that you've had to write the same (exact) code over and over, then you might want to consider consolidating that code into a shareable resource.

That way, you don't have to change 12 different files to fix a bug or add a new piece of logic.

Difficulty Adding Features

As we mentioned previously, sometimes, you are faced with the task of adding new features to your code. However, perhaps the existing code is making it really difficult to *just add* that new feature or behavior.

In these cases, refactoring can help you mold the existing code into a place where it is easy to add new behaviors!

> **Note**
>
> This also applies to architectural issues. However, this book will focus on more code-based issues.

In the End

In the end, refactoring should be a continuous and habitual activity that you have chosen to engage in.

Martin Fowler, on the topic of refactoring (https://www.refactoring.com/), said:

"Refactoring isn't a special task that would show up in a project plan. Done well, it's a regular part of programming activity."

You shouldn't have to *ask* to refactor. Just do it when it makes sense.

2

Null Checks Everywhere!

Identification

Billion-Dollar Mistake

Did you know that the inventor of the concept of *null* has called it his *Billion-Dollar Mistake* (https://www.infoq.com/presentations/Null-References-The-Billion-Dollar-Mistake-Tony-Hoare/)?

As simple as it seems, once you get into larger projects and code bases, you'll inevitably find some code that goes *off the deep end* in its use of nulls.

Sometimes, we want to simply make a property of an object optional:

```
class Product{
  public id: number;
  public title: string;
  public description: string;
}
```

In TypeScript, a **string** property can be assigned a **null** value.

But so can a **number** property!

```
const chocolate: Product = new Product();
chocolate.id = null;
chocolate.description = null;
```

Hmmm....

Example

That doesn't look so bad at first glance.

However, it can lead to the possibility of doing something like this:

```
const chocolate: Product = new Product(null, null, null);
```

What's wrong with this? Well, it allows your code (in this case, the *Product* class) to get into an inconsistent state.

Does it ever make sense to have a **Product** in your system that has no **id**? Probably not.

Ideally, as soon as you create your **Product**, it should have an **id**.

So... what happens in other places that have to deal with logic around dealing with products?

Here's the sad truth:

```
let title: string;

if(product != null) {
    if(product.id != null) {
        if(product.title != null) {
            title = product.title;
        } else {
            title = "N/A";
        }
    } else {
        title = "N/A"
```

```
    }
  } else {
      title = "N/A"
  }
```

Is *that even real code someone would write?*

Yes.

Let's look at why this code is unhealthy and considered a *code smell* before we look at some techniques to fix it.

Is It That Bad?

This code is hard to read and understand. Therefore, it's very prone to bugs when changed.

I think we can agree that having code like this scattered in your app is not ideal – especially when this kind of code is inside important, critical parts of your application!

Non-Nullable Types

As a relevant side note, someone might raise the fact that TypeScript supports non-nullable types (https://www.typescriptlang.org/docs/handbook/advanced-types.html#nullable-types).

This allows you to add a special flag to your compilation options and will prevent, by default, any variables from allowing `null` as a value.

Let's go over a few points regarding this argument:

- Most of us are dealing with existing code bases that would take *tons* of work and time to fix these compilation errors.

- Without testing the code well, and carefully avoiding assumptions, we could *still* potentially cause runtime errors by making these changes.

- This book will teach you about solutions that can be applied to other languages that may not have this option available.

Either way, it's always safer to apply smaller, more targeted improvements to our code. Again, this allows us to make sure the system still behaves the same and avoids introducing a large amount of risk when making these improvements.

Null Object Pattern

Empty Collections

Imagine you work for a company that writes software for dealing with legal cases.

As you are working on a feature, you discover some code:

```
const legalCases: LegalCase[] = await fetchCasesFromAPI();
for (const legalCase of legalCases) {
    if(legalCase.documents != null) {
        uploadDocuments(legalCase.documents);
    }
}
```

Remember that we should be wary of null checks? What if some other part of the code forgot to check for a *null* array?

The Null Object pattern can help: you create an object that represents an *empty* or **null** object.

Fixing It Up

Let's look at the **fetchCasesFromAPI()** method. We'll apply a version of this pattern that's a very common practice in JavaScript and TypeScript when dealing with arrays:

```
const fetchCasesFromAPI = async function() {
    const legalCases: LegalCase[] = await $http.get('legal-cases/');

    for (const legalCase of legalCases) {
        // Null Object Pattern
        legalCase.documents = legalCase.documents || [];
    }
    return legalCases;
}
```

Instead of leaving empty arrays/collections as **null**, we are assigning them an actual empty array.

Now, no one else will need to make a null check!

But what about the entire legal case collection itself? What if the API returns **null**?

```
const fetchCasesFromAPI = async function() {
    const legalCasesFromAPI: LegalCase[] = await $http.get('legal-cases/');
    // Null Object Pattern
```

```
    const legalCases = legalCasesFromAPI || [];

    for (const legalCase of legalCases) {
        // Null Object Pattern
        legalCase.documents = legalCase.documents || [];
    }
    return legalCases;
}
```

Cool!

Now, we've made sure that everyone who uses this method doesn't need to be worried about checking for nulls.

Take 2

Other languages, such as C#, Java, and so on, won't allow you to assign a mere empty array to a collection due to rules about strong typing.

In those cases, you can use something like this version of the Null Object pattern:

```
class EmptyArray<T> {
    static create<T>() {
        return new Array<T>()
    }
}

// Use it like this:
const myEmptyArray: string[] = EmptyArray.create<string>();
```

What About Objects?

Imagine that you are working on a video game. In it, some levels might have a boss.

When checking whether the current level has a boss, you might see something like this:

```
if(currentLevel.boss != null) {
    currentLevel.boss.fight(player);
}
```

We might find other places that do this null check:

```
if(currentLevel.boss != null) {
    currentLevel.completed = currentLevel.boss.isDead();
}
```

If we introduce a **null** object, then we can simply remove all these null checks.

First, we need an interface to represent our **Boss**:

```
interface IBoss {
    fight(player: Player);
    isDead();
}
```

Then, we can create our concrete boss class:

```
class Boss implements IBoss {
    fight(player: Player) {
        // Do some logic and return a bool.
    }

    isDead() {
        // Return whether boss is dead depending on how the fight went.
    }
}
```

Next, we'll create an implementation of the **IBoss** interface that represents a *null* **Boss**:

```
class NullBoss implements IBoss {
    fight(player: Player) {
        // Player always wins.
    }
    isDead() {
        return true;
    }
}
```

NullBoss will automatically allow the player to *win*, and we can remove all our null checks!

In the following code example, if the boss is an instance of **NullBoss** or **Boss**, no extra checks need to be made:

```
currentLevel.boss.fight(player);
currentLevel.boss.isDead();
```

Special Case Pattern

Situation

Imagine there's a scheduled background process that fetches multiple orders from your database and tries to place/finalize them.

Like Amazon, we might have a complex process around placing orders that isn't as linear as we might think it would be.

In this case, we want a buffer period between the time when you click *place order* and when the order is *really* placed. This will make canceling an order an easy process (it avoids having to remove credit card charges and so on).

Given this scenario, we might be trying to process orders that have already been changed to an alternate state:

- Canceled order.

- Payment declined.

- The payment gateway is not responding, so we need to wait and retry later.

- Others!

Whenever you have multiple versions of these kinds of *special* cases, the Special Case pattern is here to save the day!

This pattern is just like the Null Object pattern but takes it that extra step.

An Order Class That Needs to Be Refactored

Imagine you come across this class, which represents the orders in your code:

```
class Order {
    constructor() {
    }

    public placeOrder() {
        // Do some stuff...
    }
}
```

Your business now tells you that they need the kind of process that was described at the beginning of this section.

Many developers would do something like this:

```
enum OrderStatus {
    Pending, FraudulentAccount, PaymentRejected
}

class Order {
    public status: OrderStatus;

    constructor() {
    }

    public placeOrder() {
        // Do some stuff...
    }
}
```

And somewhere else, they would do something like this:

```
if(order.status === OrderStatus.Pending) {
    order.placeOrder();
} else if(order.status === OrderStatus.PaymentRejected) {
    // Something else...
}
// And on and on...
```

Each of these states (**Pending**, **Incomplete**, **FraudulentAccount**, and **PaymentRejected**) still need to attempt to place the order. They each require different ways or extra steps in the process.

How do we solve this in a cleaner way?

Refactoring the Order Class

Using the *Special Case* pattern, we can create special versions of the **Order** class.

First, we create an interface for the order: **IOrder**.

Next, let's create some of these special case classes:

```
class PendingOrder implements IOrder {
    constructor() {
    }

    public placeOrder() {
        // API call, etc.
    }
}

class PaymentRejectedOrder implements IOrder {
    constructor() {
    }

    public placeOrder() {
        // Try to pay again. Etc.
    }
}

class OrderOnFraudulentAccount implements IOrder {
    constructor() {
    }

    public placeOrder() {
        // Notify the fraud department. The actual order placement will be
        // decided and placed by the fraud department.
    }
}
```

Given these changes, we might even want to rename the **placeOrder** method to **tryPlaceOrder** for more semantic correctness.

Somewhere else in our code, we might have a function that gives us instances of any orders that need to be placed (which could be any type of special case class we created):

```
const ordersCollection: IOrder[] = await getOrders();
for(const order of ordersCollection) {
    order.placeOrder();
}
```

Since we've exposed all our orders via an interface, there's no need to figure out what the status of the class is! Each individual class will just *know* what it needs to do.

3

Wordy Conditionals

Identification

A Little Bit of This, a Little Bit of That

If you work as a professional software developer, then you *must* have seen code like this before. Truth be told... we've all *written* code like this before:

```
if(user.role === "admin"
    && user.isActive
    && user.permissions.some(p => p === "edit")) {

    // Do stuff
}
```

I know you've seen this before – *and versions of this that are much worse and more complex!*

These long lists of conditionals we find inside our **if** statements can be called *verbose conditionals*:

- They are hard to read.

- They are hard to understand once you've read them.

- They are hard to modify.

- They are hard to test (well... you can't really directly test them at all).

Misbehaving Conditionals

These lengthy conditionals often lead to software that will misbehave and not work the way you would want it to.

More often than not, when we find bugs in these places, we usually try to quickly add a fix, move on, and forget about it.

Then, another similar piece of code causes a bug the next week!

Finally, you realize it was actually the exact same logic copied and pasted – so you actually didn't fix the root issue!

The next section will help you tame these wild conditionals!

Combining Conditionals

Situation

In the following sections of this chapter, we are going to stick with the same example as the code snippet in the previous section. We'll improve it one step at a time.

Often, this is how you will approach refactoring: starting with the simplest refactoring. As your code becomes more complex or requires more TLC, then you can bring out *the big guns*.

Our scenario is a web application where we need to check some user permissions around editing a resource.

The Code

```
if(user.role === "admin"
    && user.active
    && user.permissions.some(p => p === "edit")) {

    // Do stuff.
}
```

How can we make this more readable, understandable, less prone to bugs, and easier to maintain?

One of the *quick* wins you can get with these kinds of verbose conditionals is to start by moving each one into its own variable.

Let's start with this:

```
const isAdmin: boolean = user.role === "admin";
const userIsActive: boolean = user.active;
const userCanEdit: boolean = user.permissions.some(p => p === "edit");
```

Next, let's introduce a new variable that will combine the meaning of what we are trying to achieve in the first place, and use it in our **if** statement:

```
const activeAdminCanEdit: boolean = isAdmin && userIsActive && userCanEdit;

if (activeAdminCanEdit) {
    // Do stuff.
}
```

Since we've named our variables very clearly and explicitly, this is much easier to understand.

Guideline

As a general guideline, try to make your **if** statements refer to the condition of *one* variable. If you are checking multiple variables, then consider combining them into a new one that will add more clarity and semantic meaning.

Extracting Methods from Conditionals

Consider the code we had in the previous section:

```
const isAdmin: boolean = user.role === "admin";
const userIsActive: boolean = user.active;
const userCanEdit: boolean = user.permissions.some(p => p === "edit");

const activeAdminCanEdit: boolean = isAdmin && userIsActive && userCanEdit;

if(activeAdminCanEdit) {
    // Do stuff.
}
```

In some cases, the above code is fine.

In other cases, sometimes, you just get that feeling... something's not right.

What's Wrong Here?

Let's think through this code.

Is it possible that somewhere else in our application we will need to check whether:

- A user is an admin?

- A user is active?

- A user can edit certain resources?

The answer is... probably... *yes.*

Right now, is that logic able to be accessed by other parts of your application?

Nope.

Oh, yeah. There's another thing. All of these conditionals are performed in relation to your user.

The Fix

Why don't we take the logic from those conditionals and extract them as methods on our user class? Since these methods are performing logic that's *about* the user, it makes sense to give our user object ownership of these behaviors/states.

If we did that, we would get:

```
const activeAdminCanEdit: boolean = user.isAdmin()
    && user.isActive()
    && user.canEdit();

if(activeAdminCanEdit) {
    // Do stuff.
}
```

That looks a bit better. But more importantly, you can share these pieces, which might be needed by other parts of your application!

Extracting Conditional Logic to Explicit Classes

In the previous section, we looked at extracting conditional logic as new methods on a user object.

Sometimes, though, we end up doing this refactoring over and over.

What we are left with is a **User** class that is *filled* with tons of these kinds of methods.

> **Note**
>
> This can be an issue that is best solved by actually modeling your classes using a domain-driven design approach.
>
> While being beyond what this book covers, you might be interested in looking into the concept of bounded contexts (https://www.martinfowler.com/bliki/BoundedContext.html).

Let's Get Classy

Imagine that our **User** class looked something like this now:

```
class User {
    isAdmin(): boolean { /* Code */ }

    isActive(): boolean { /* Code */ }

    canEdit(): boolean { /* Code */ }
    isActiveAdmin(): boolean { /* Code */ }
```

```
    isActiveAdminThatCanEdit(): boolean { /* Code */ }

    // And dozens of more methods...
}
```

You can tell that this kind of stuff will get much harder to maintain over time since the number of methods is exploding!

Let's take the **isActiveAdmin** method, for example. What if we extracted this as an entirely new class? What would that look like?

```
class UserIsActiveAdmin {
    private _user: User;

    constructor(user: User) {
        this._user = user;
    }

    public invoke(): boolean {
        return this._user.isAdmin()
            && this._user.isActive();
    }
}
```

SRP

In essence, we've just applied the Single Responsibility Principle, or SRP (https://deviq. com/single-responsibility-principle/), to our code.

Our **User** class *doesn't* have that method anymore, so it's smaller and therefore easier to understand and read.

The new class we've made deals with one specific responsibility and is therefore much more maintainable.

Using It

Using the new class would look like this:

```
const activeAdminCanEdit: boolean = new UserIsActiveAdmin(user).invoke()
    && user.canEdit();

if(activeAdminCanEdit) {
    // Do stuff.
}
```

Now we get the benefits of:

- Having our logic sharable with other parts of our application
- Our **User** class not becoming a dumping ground for methods
- Our conditional logic still benefiting from the simplification of our code

Pipe Classes

In the last section, we created a new class, **UserIsActiveAdmin**, and ended up with this:

```
const activeAdminCanEdit: boolean = new UserIsActiveAdmin(user).invoke()
    && user.canEdit();

if(activeAdminCanEdit) {
    // Do stuff.
}
```

Building these kinds of classes that deal with a single *test* or condition helps us to build lots of smaller pieces that we can later combine together for more complex scenarios.

This refactoring is useful, but I want to show you an even more flexible way to build these classes.

Your Classes Might Be Doing Too Much...

Looking at the code sample at the beginning of the chapter, what if we wanted to further combine *all* the logic into a single class?

We might call it **UserIsActiveAdminAndCanEdit**. Okay.

And that might be fine. But what if we have, let's say, eight different conditionals we need to check here?

Our class might have this name:

CheckOneCheckTwoCheckThreeCheckFourCheckFiveCheckSixCheckSevenCheckEight

Ouch. Probably not a good thing to do.

What *can* we do then?

Piping Our Logic

If your code base is getting to this point, then I suggest that you *keep these individual classes limited to checking one or two things.*

Next, we can create a common interface:

```
interface IPipeableCondition {
    check(): boolean;
}
```

Each one of these classes will implement the interface, as in this example:

```
class UserIsActiveAdmin implements IPipeableCondition {
    private _user: User;

    constructor(user: User) {
        this._user = user;
    }

    public check(): boolean {
        return this._user.isAdmin()
            && this._user.isActive();
    }
}
```

Imagine we had a good number of these classes. We could combine them together in a collection and *pipe* them all through a mechanism that makes sure all of them *pass*:

```
const conditions: IPipeableCondition[] = [
    new UserIsActiveAdmin(user),
    new UserCanEdit(user),
    new UserIsNotBlacklisted(user),
    new UserLivesInAvailableLocation(user)
];

const valid = conditions.every(p => p.check());

if(valid) {
    // Do stuff.
}
```

We've created a pipe where we can specify what items are applicable and they will all automatically be combined at runtime.

This is usually not the *go-to* when designing your code. But it's good to know that it's an option – and when your code warrants it, it's a great way to simplify things.

Bonus Refactor

If we were going to use these pipes in multiple places in our app, then we would want to build another class that was responsible for the piping logic:

```
class ConditionsPipe {
    private _conditions: IPipeableCondition[];

    constructor(conditions: IPipeableCondition[]) {
        this._conditions = conditions;
    }

    check(): boolean {
        return this._conditions.every(p => p.check());
    }
}
```

We would use it like this:

```
const pipe = new ConditionsPipe([
    new UserIsActiveAdmin(user),
    new UserCanEdit(user),
    new UserIsNotBlacklisted(user),
    new UserLivesInAvailableLocation(user)
]);

if(pipe.check()) {
    // Do stuff.
}
```

Nested Conditionals

Identification

A Monster

I once worked on a project that had a particular function with ~ 5,000 lines of code in it.

Yes – one function with about 5,000 lines of code.

Welcome to the real world.

Inside this function was basically one massive `switch` statement with lots of nested `if` statements.

It was *really* hard to understand.

Code like this is really common, though. One day, a developer comes along and adds a couple more conditionals. Another day, someone adds a few more. Next thing you know, it's a huge mess of nested conditionals that no one understands anymore.

A Closer Look

These nested conditionals can look something like this:

```
let result: OrderResult = null;

if(!order.wasCancelled()) {
    if(order.isPaid()) {
        result = order.sendToShipping();
    } else {
        if(order.isFraudulent()) {
            result = order.sendToFraudDept();
        } else {
            result = order.tryAgainLater();
        }
    }
}

return result;
```

By looking really closely, you can try to figure out what it's doing.

But it's very clear – *that it is not easy to read or understand.*

This type of code can easily lead to bugs and unintended behavior.

In the next few sections, we'll have a look at a few ways to slay this monster!

Guard Clauses

Scenario

In this section (and the next), we're working on a backend system that processes orders for a large e-commerce platform.

We're working with code in a background process that needs to check whether an order was paid, canceled, is suspected of fraud, and so on.

As we'll see, it's a little hard to work with due to containing nested conditionals.

Fail Fast

One of the best ways to deal with nested conditionals is to create what are called **guard clauses** (https://refactoring.com/catalog/replaceNestedConditionalWithGuardClauses.html).

In essence, we want to follow a couple of guiding principles:

- Return from our method at the earliest time possible.

- Each condition (if possible) is tested to see whether it fails rather than passes.

Both of these principles combined are sometimes termed *fail fast*. We want our methods to *fail* as fast as possible. When our code contains nested conditionals, we are doing the opposite!

Fixing It Up

Consider this code:

```
let result = null;

if(!order.wasCancelled()) {
    if(order.isPaid()) {
        result = order.sendToShipping();
    } else {
        if(order.isFraudulent()) {
            result = order.sendToFraudDept();
        } else {
            result = order.tryAgainLater();
        }
    }
}

return result;
```

Let's take each condition and turn it into one check that tries to fail fast.

First, we'll check whether the order was canceled. If it was, we want to simply ignore the rest of the function and fail fast:

```
if(order.wasCancelled()) {
    return;
}
```

Let's check whether the order was already paid and return from our function immediately:

```
if(order.wasPaid()) {
    return order.sendToShipping();
}
```

And so on. At the end, we'll end up with:

```
if(order.wasCancelled()) {
    return;
}

if(order.wasPaid()) {
    return order.sendToShipping();
}

if(order.isFraudulent()) {
    return order.sendToFraudDept();
}

return order.tryAgainLater();
```

Now that our code is flat, it's much easier to read and understand. This will lead to code that is less error-prone, easier to understand, and way simpler to extend if we need to add some new logic.

Gate Classes

Gate classes is a term I've used to name a certain pattern that I use in certain contexts.

At times, you have code where you don't want the rest of the function to run at all unless certain conditions are met (such as guard clauses):

```
if(!order.wasCancelled()) {
    // A bunch of code that does stuff.

    if(!order.isFraudlent()) {
        // Some more code.
    }
}
```

Notice that we have two conditionals (one being nested) and they are *not* followed by **else** or **else if**.

They make one check and act as a gate, as it were, to the rest of the code inside that **if** statement.

That's why I like to call these kinds of statement *gates* since they only let the rest of the code run if the gate is *opened up*.

Scenario

Here's the situation we're going to address. It's similar to the code above, but now we have some repositories that are being used to fetch data to conduct our checks:

```
const accountIsVerified = await accountRepo.accountIsVerified(userAccount);
const canPlaceOrder = await orderRepo.userCanPlaceOrder(user);

if(accountIsVerified) {
    if(canPlaceOrder) {
        await orderRepo.placeOrder(order);
    }
}
```

We've got **if** statements that act as gates to the code that needs to run. But, in this case, our code has external dependencies (the repositories).

One more thing – we need to do these checks in *other places in our application!*

How can we make these checks more explicit, sharable, and maintainable?

Gate Classes to the Rescue

We can create *gate classes* by extracting each condition to a new class. These will throw an exception upon failure.

> **Note**
> Keep reading to understand why we will throw exceptions.

Here's our first gate class:

```
class AccountIsVerifiedGate {
    private _accountRepo: AccountRepo;

    constructor(accountRepo: AccountRepo) {
        this._accountRepo = accountRepo;
    }

    async invoke(account: UserAccount) {
```

```
        const isVerified = await this._accountRepo.accountIsVerified(account);
        if(!isVerified) {
            throw "Gate exception";
        }
    }
}
```

Next, we will create one called **UserCanPlaceOrderGate**, too.

Now, in our refactored code, we have:

```
// Both gate classes are supplied as external dependencies.

await accountIsVerifiedGate.invoke(userAccount);
await userCanPlaceOrderGate.invoke(user);
await orderRepo.placeOrder(order);
```

If any of the gate classes fail, then they will throw an exception and therefore leave the running method.

Somewhere up the stack, we would want to enable some type of global error handler that would catch a specific type of exception (which we didn't create in this example) and deal with it accordingly.

Useful for Web APIs

This pattern is useful in Web APIs, for example. When a gate class fails and throws a special type of exception, a middleware will send back a specific HTTP status, such as 401 or 403, automatically for you.

This is not an entry-level pattern to use, but in situations like those above, they can make your code much easier to understand and reason about. And, you can automate what happens when they fail.

5

Primitive Overuse

Identification

One of the classic *code smells* is called primitive overuse.

It's deceptively simple.

Take this code, for example:

```
const email: string = user.email;

if(email !== null && email !== "") {
    // Do something with the email.
}
```

Notice that we are handling the email's raw data?

Or, consider this:

```
const firstname = user.firstname || "";
const lastname = user.lastname || "";
const fullName: string = firstname + " " + lastname;
```

Notice all that extra checking around making sure the user's names are not **null**? You've seen code like this, no doubt.

What's Wrong Here?

What's wrong with this code? There are a few things to think about:

- That logic is not sharable and therefore will be duplicated all over the place.

- In more complex scenarios, it's hard to see what the underlying business concept represents (which leads to code that's hard to understand).

- If there is an underlying business concept, it's implicit, not explicit.

The business concept in the code example above is something like a user's *display name* or *full name*.

However, that concept only exists temporarily in a variable *that just happened to be named correctly*. Will it be named the same thing in other places? If you have other developers on your team, *probably not*.

We have code that's potentially hard to grasp from a business perspective, hard to understand in complex scenarios, and not sharable to other places in your application.

Let's look through some solutions in the following sections!

Value Objects

Scenario

We've been working on email logic for a Software-as-a-Service (SaaS) product. Lately, working with this part of the code base has caused inadvertent bugs to appear.

We've decided that now is a good time to reach in, clean it up, and improve its overall quality.

From a high-level perspective, our code is checking whether an email address is sent to a specific internal domain (such as *internal-company.com*). If the username (that is, the email address' *local-part*) is *info*, then we send the email to our internal customer support team. Otherwise, we just send it to the intended recipient.

Here's our code:

```
const domain: string = email.replace(/.*@/, "");
const userName = email.replace(domain, "");

const sendInternal: boolean = domain === "internal-company.com";
if(sendInternal) {
    if(userName === "info") {
        mailer.sendToCustomerServiceTeam(email, message);
    } else {
        mailer.mailToInternalServer(email, message);
    }
} else {
    throw "Cannot email externally.";
}
```

Initial Refactor

First, we want to take care of the nested conditionals. There's an entire section on this earlier in the book.

After applying those techniques, we might end up with this:

```
const domain: string = email.replace(/.*@/, "");
const userName = email.replace(domain, "");

const sendExternal: boolean = domain !== "internal-company.com";

if(sendExternal) {
    throw "Cannot email externally.";
}

if(userName === "info") {
    mailer.sendToCustomerServiceTeam(email, message);
    return;
}

mailer.mailToInternalServer(email, message);
```

There are still all these inline conditions that just don't feel right, though...

Addressing Primitives

The biggest issue is that there is an underlying concept of an *email address*. But, it's implicit – not explicit.

We're treating the **string** variable holding the raw data of the email address as our primary focus and sprinkling the logic for it everywhere.

Instead, we need to consolidate/encapsulate this business concept and its associated logic into a new kind of object.

Creating Our Object

First, let's create a class:

```
class EmailAddress {
    private _value: string;

    constructor(value: string) {
        this._value = value;
    }
}
```

That's a good start.

Let's put all our logic into this class now.

We are going to build a specific kind of object, called a **value object**. Value objects have certain properties that we'll go over as we progress through this chapter:

```
class EmailAddress {
    private _value: string;
    private _domain: string;
    private _userName: string

    constructor(value: string) {
        this._value = value;
        this._domain: string = value.replace(/.*@/, "");
        this._userName = value.replace(domain, "");
    }

    isExternal(): boolean {
        return this._domain !== "internal-company.com";
    }

    isInfoUser(): boolean {
```

```
            return this._userName === "info";
        }

    value() {
        return this._value;
    }
}
```

Notice that we only expose pieces of data that will be needed by the outside world. Always be careful about what you expose.

One rule around value objects is that they cannot be modified once instantiated (that is, they are immutable). We only expose read-only methods that give other parts of our application information about the email address. But no one is allowed to change our object.

Creating classes that are immutable makes our code easier to predict, test, and reason about. Many bugs and readability issues arise from classes that modify their internal state in different ways. Worse still are classes that expose their internal properties and let the outside world change them! This leads to code that is *really* unpredictable!

Moving Along

Going back to the original code we were refactoring, we get this:

```
const emailAddress: EmailAddress = new EmailAddress(email);

if(emailAddress.isExternal()) {
    throw "Cannot email externally.";
}

if(emailAddress.isInfoUser()) {
    mailer.sendToCustomerServiceTeam(emailAddress.value(), message);
    return;
}

mailer.mailToInternalServer(emailAddress.value(), message);
```

That seems much clearer. But, there's another sneaky issue here.

We can create an email address that, according to our system, is *invalid*. According to our business rules, any email address that doesn't have the domain *internal-company. com* is technically not valid and cannot be emailed.

For example, it could happen that another developer does something like this:

```
const emailAddress: EmailAddress = new EmailAddress("this_is_invalid@gmail.
com");

mailer.mailToInternalServer(emailAddress.value(), message);
```

Oops!

Immediate Validation

Our **value** object is not a *true* value object. True value objects can *never* be in an invalid or inconsistent state.

One common way to enforce this is to perform validation in the constructor, then throw exceptions on any errors:

```
constructor(value: string) {
    if(this.isExternal(value)) {
        throw "Cannot email externally.";
    }

    // Other code when this object is valid.
}
```

Now we get:

```
try {
    const emailAddress: EmailAddress = new EmailAddress(email);
    doEmailLogic(emailAddress);
} catch(Exception e) {
    // Do stuff.
}

function doEmailLogic(emailAddress: EmailAddress) : void {
    if(emailAddress.isInfoUser()) {
        mailer.sendToCustomerServiceTeam(emailAddress.value(), message);
        return;
    }

    mailer.mailToInternalServer(emailAddress.value(), message);
}
```

We've combined guard clauses and value objects to create some code that is going to be easier to read and will avoid other developers misusing our class.

Deceptive Booleans

We've been looking at some of the issues around using primitive types too often.

Primitive types should be the building blocks out of which we create more useful business-oriented concepts/abstractions in our code.

Again, this helps each specific business concept to have all of its logic in one place (which means we can share it and reason about it much more easily), implement more robust error handling, reduce bugs, and so on.

In this section, I want to look at the most common cause of primitive overuse that I've experienced. I see it *all the time*.

Like many of our code smells, it's deceptively simple at first glance.

Scenario

In our scenario, we're working on a web application that helps clients to sell their used items online.

We've been asked to add some extra rules around the part of our system that authenticates users.

Right now, the system only checks whether a user was successfully authenticated:

```
const isAuthenticated: boolean = await userIsAuthenticated(username, password);

if(isAuthenticated) {
    redirectToUserDashboard();
} else {
    returnErrorOnLoginPage("Credentials are not valid.");
}
```

New Business Rules

Our company now wants us to check whether users are active. Inactive users will not be able to log in.

Many developers would do something like this:

```
const user: User = await userIsAuthenticated(username, password);
const isAuthenticated: boolean = user !== null;


if(isAuthenticated) {
    if(user.isActive) {
        redirectToUserDashboard();
    } else {
        returnErrorOnLoginPage("User is not active.");
    }
} else {
    returnErrorOnLoginPage("Credentials are not valid.");
}
```

Oh no! We've introduced code smells that we know are going to cause maintainability issues.

We've got some null checks and nested conditions in there now.

So, let's refactor that first by applying (a) the special case pattern and (b) guard clauses:

```
// This will now always return a User, but it may be a special case type
// of User that will return false for "user.isAuthenticated()", etc.
const user: User = await userIsAuthenticated(username, password);

// We've created guard clauses here.
if(!user.isAuthenticated()) {
    returnErrorOnLoginPage("Credentials are not valid.");
}

if(!user.isActive()) {
    returnErrorOnLoginPage("User is not active.");
}

redirectToUserDashboard();
```

Much better.

More Rules...

Now that your managers have seen how fast you were able to add that new business rule, they have a few more they need:

- If the user's session already exists, then send the user to a special home page.
- If the user has locked their account due to too many login attempts, send them to a special page.
- If this is a user's first login, then send them to a special welcome page.

Yikes!

> **Note**
>
> If you've been in the industry for a few years, then you know how common this is!

At first glance, we might do something naïve:

```
// This will now always return a User, but it may be a special case type
// of User that will return false for "user.isAuthenticated()", etc.
const user: User = await userIsAuthenticated(username, password);

// We've created guard clauses here.
if(!user.isAuthenticated()) {
    returnErrorOnLoginPage("Credentials are not valid.");
}

if(!user.isActive()) {
    returnErrorOnLoginPage("User is not active.");
}

if(user.alreadyHadSession()) {
    redirectToHomePage();
}

if(user.isLockedOut()) {
    redirectToUserLockedOutPage();
}
```

```
if(user.isFirstLogin()) {
    redirectToWelcomePage();
}
```

```
redirectToUserDashboard();
```

Notice that because we introduced guard clauses, it's much easier to add new logic here? That's one of the awesome benefits of making your code high-quality – it leads to future changes being *much* easier to change and add new logic to.

But, in this case, there's an issue. Can you spot it?

Our **User** class is becoming a dumping ground for all our authentication logic.

Is It Really That Bad?

Is it that bad? *Yep.*

Think about it: what other places in your app will need this data? Nowhere – it's all authentication logic.

One refactoring would be to create a new class called **AuthenticatedUser** and put only authentication-related logic in that class.

This would follow the **single responsibility principle**.

But, there's a much simpler fix we could use.

Just Use Enums

Any time I see this pattern (the result of a method is either a Boolean or an object that has Booleans that are checked immediately), it's a much better practice to replace the Booleans with an enum.

From our last code snippet above, let's change the **userIsAuthenticated** method to something that more accurately describes what we are trying to do: **tryAuthenticateUser**.

And, instead of returning either a Boolean or a user, we'll just send back an enum that tells us exactly what the results were since that's all we are interested in knowing:

```
enum AuthenticationResult {
    InvalidCredentials,
    UserIsNotActive,
```

```
    HasExistingSession,
    IsLockedOut,
    IsFirstLogin,
    Successful
}
```

There's our new enum, which will specify all the possible results from attempting to authenticate a user.

Next, we'll use that enum:

```
const result: AuthenticationResult = await tryAuthenticateUser(username,
password);

if(result === AuthenticationResult.InvalidCredentials) {
    returnErrorOnLoginPage("Credentials are not valid.");
}

if(result === AuthenticationResult.UserIsNotActive) {
    returnErrorOnLoginPage("User is not active.");
}

if(result === AuthenticationResult.HasExistingSession) {
    redirectToHomePage();
}

if(result === AuthenticationResult.IsLockedOut) {
    redirectToUserLockedOutPage();
}

if(result === AuthenticationResult.IsFirstLogin) {
    redirectToWelcomePage();
}

redirectToUserDashboard();
```

Notice how much more readable that is? And, we aren't polluting our **User** class anymore with a bunch of extra data that is unnecessary.

We are returning *one value*. This is a great way to simplify your code.

This is one of my favorite refactorings! I hope you will find it useful, too.

Strategy Pattern

Whenever I use this refactoring, I automatically know that the strategy pattern might help me some more.

Imagine the code above had *lots* more business rules and paths.

We could further simplify it by using a form of the strategy pattern:

```
const strategies: any = [];

strategies[AuthenticationResult.InvalidCredentials] =
    () => returnErrorOnLoginPage("Credentials are not valid.");
strategies[AuthenticationResult.UserIsNotActive] =
    () => returnErrorOnLoginPage("User is not active.");
strategies[AuthenticationResult.HasExistingSession] =
    () => redirectToHomePage();
strategies[AuthenticationResult.IsLockedOut] =
    () => redirectToUserLockedOutPage();
strategies[AuthenticationResult.IsFirstLogin] =
    () => redirectToWelcomePage();
strategies[AuthenticationResult.Successful] =
    () => redirectToUserDashboard();

strategies[result]();
```

Lengthy Method Signatures

Identification

Imagine a method that fetches all active users from a database:

```
public getUsers() : User[] {
    // Does stuff.
}
```

A business came to you with some new features they need. You'll need to reuse the same logic from the previous method. But now it needs to include all *inactive* users.

What's the easy fix? Something like this?

```
public getUsers(includeInactive: boolean = false) : User[] {

}
```

The Slippery Slope of Optional Parameters

That's a seemingly crafty fix. It ensures you won't duplicate that logic somewhere else by copying and pasting it.

Over time, however, this can slowly grow into a grossly unmaintainable method.

Imagine that, over the next few weeks, several junior developers add some new features to this method.

You find that this method signature has exploded and become this:

```
public getUsers(
    includeInactive: boolean = false,
    filterText: string = null,
    orderByName: boolean = false,
    forHireDate: Date = null) : User[] {
}
```

If you've been involved in any real-world projects that had methods to fetch data from a backend database, then you've probably seen this a ton of times.

> **Note**
>
> I've worked on a real-world project that has a method like this with ~50 parameters!

The Issue

Anyone who's dealt with these kinds of methods with all these extra optional parameters knows that they are not maintainable. They are hard to understand because they do so many different things!

And, as we'll see in the next chapter, how do we know if changing one parameter will affect another? What if filtering the user by their name should only apply to active users? How can we know that by simply looking at the method signature?

These methods also signal to other less experienced developers that this is a *good practice* and a good way to add new functionality (which is not true).

Even if you don't have optional parameters, having a method with many required parameters is a sign that your method is probably doing too much (see the Single Responsibility Principle: https://deviq.com/single-responsibility-principle/).

Guidelines

Ideally, you want your methods to have just a few parameters at most. And, if at all possible, you should try to avoid optional parameters.

Again, these aren't hard-and-fast rules, but they are guidelines that, if followed, will ensure you don't cause issues down the road.

Let's look at fixing some of these unhealthy methods!

Creating a Reusable Private Method

The code snippet from the previous chapter is such a common case that we'll use it in this section:

```
public getUsers(
    includeInactive: boolean = false,
    filterText: string = null,
    orderByName: boolean = false,
    forHireDate: Date = null) : User[] {
}
```

Ask yourself: *Are the parameters just data that I need to give it? Or do some of the parameters indicate that the method is going to alter its behavior?*

If you answered *yes* to the second question, then you probably want to refactor this method.

The easy wins when finding these kinds of methods is to:

1. Make them private

2. Create wrapper methods exposing the intended behaviors by their individual names

Step 1 would entail changing **getUsers** to a private method.

Next, let's look at all the different behaviors this method is exposing:

- Get active users

- Get inactive users

- Get users that have a certain name

- Get users and order them by their name

- Get users that have a specific hire date

Here's why these methods are *so bad* – any combination of *all* those behaviors might be true too!

For example:

- Get active users and users that have a specific hire date
- Get inactive users and users named `James` and order them by their name
- And so on

While the code inside the method *may not combine all the behaviors*, as a user of this method, how can you know that?

You can open the method's source code and try to figure it out?

But that's *really bad.* If you have to open up the source code of a method to understand how to use it, then that method has failed to give you a clear, understandable, and usable abstraction.

Methods, when written well, should be easy to use and understand when they are appropriate.

A Simple Example

You may open up the source code for this method – which only has four parameters – and discovers that it has dozens of combinations of these parameters!

A method that *only has four optional parameters* is still *really* tricky.

We'll assume for our example that these parameters were coded in a way that they didn't interact with each other that much.

Here are the kinds of behaviors we'll need to expose:

- Get active/inactive users
- Get active users, filtering by their name
- Get active users, filtering by their name and ordering the results by name
- Get active users that have a specific hire date

Creating Semantically Meaningful Methods

Let's take each of those required behaviors and create some methods for them:

```
// Here's our "main" private method
private getUsers(
    includeInactive: boolean = false,
    filterText: string = null,
    orderByName: boolean = false,
    forHireDate: Date = null) : User[] {
}

public getActiveUsers() : User[] {
    return getUsers(false);
}

public getInactiveUsers() : User[] {
    return getUsers(true);
}

public getActiveUsersByName(filter: string) : User[] {
    return getUsers(false, filter);
}

public getActiveUsersOrderedAndFilteredByName(filter: string) : User[] {
    return getUsers(false, filter, true);
}

public getActiveUsersForHireDate(hireDate: Date) : User[] {
    return getUsers(false, null, false, hireDate);
}
```

Now, whenever you go to use these methods, it will be *very clear* what each method does. They will be easy to use.

These new methods also avoid the user/caller having to make assumptions about how the private method works under the covers.

A Brief Look at Some Advanced Solutions

As an alternative solution, you might want to consider using a fluent approach.

> **Note**
>
> I've written about fluent interfaces at https://dev.to/jamesmh/fluent-apis-make-developers-love-using-your-libraries-2d7c, if you're interested.

Based on the preceding example, when using this pattern, you might end up with something like this:

```
public getActiveUsersOrderedAndFilteredByName(filter: string) : User[] {
    return new UserQuery()
        .filterByName(filter);
        .orderByName();
        .execute();
}

public getActiveUsersForHireDate(hireDate: Date) : User[] {
    return new UserQuery()
        .forHireDate(hireDate)
        .execute();
}
```

If your project is such that you need to use database query methods quite a bit, then building something more generic might work. That might look like this in use:

```
public getActiveUsersOrderedAndFilteredByName(filter: string) : User[] {
    return new UserQueryBuilder()
        .whereLike("Username", filter)
        .orderBy("Username")
        .execute();
}

public getActiveUsersForHireDate(hireDate: Date) : User[] {
    return new UserQueryBuilder()
        .where("HireDate", hireDate)
        .execute();
}
```

Chances are, your framework/language already has a library to do this for you:

- .NET's Entity Framework (https://docs.microsoft.com/en-us/ef/)
- .NET's Dapper (https://github.com/StackExchange/Dapper)
- Java's Hibernate (https://hibernate.org/)
- PHP's Doctrine (https://www.doctrine-project.org/)
- TypeScript's TypeORM (https://github.com/typeorm/typeorm)

> **Note**
>
> In some more advanced cases, you might even want to look into the Specification Pattern. For a primer, visit https://matt.berther.io/2005/03/25/the-specification-pattern-a-primer/, and for a more in-depth explanation, visit https://enterprisecraftsmanship.com/2016/02/08/specification-pattern-c-implementation/.

Extracting Data Objects

Some methods have many parameters. As we saw in the previous section, sometimes that's due to optional parameters that *tell* the method to behave in an alternative way.

Other times, we are just passing a lot of data through to the method.

Here's an example of this scenario:

```
public async saveUserDetails(
    id: number,
    employeeId: string,
    firstName: string,
    lastName: string,
    emailAddress: string,
    phone: string,
    fax: string,
    ) : Promise<void> {
    // Save the data.
}
```

You might use it like this:

```
await saveUserDetails(id, empId, firstName, lastName, emailAddress, phone, fax);
```

That's a lot of individual variables that we need to be aware of.

> **Note**
>
> If you've read the chapter on primitive overuse, you might notice that we are using primitive types everywhere. One way to make this better would be to create value objects!

These parameters are not telling the method to behave in a certain way (like in the previous section), but are just pieces of data that we need to process or work with.

As it happens, all the parameters are related to a user's information, which we need to store.

Extraction

In cases like this, it's best to take all the pieces of data and extract a new kind of object. It will be used as an easier and more maintainable way of supplying data to this method.

Let's create a new class called **UserForStorage**. This name explicitly tells other developers that this object is specifically used for storing a user's information – nothing else.

```
class UserForStorage {
    id: number;
    employeeId: string;
    firstName: string;
    lastName: string;
    emailAddress: string;
    phone: string;
    fax: string;
}
```

Given our context, this may be the best thing to do. In other cases, you may want to use a more generic **user** class. It depends on your application, its size, how it's architected, how much isolation you want, and so on. I tend to prefer more isolation in my code.

You might want to add a constructor to that, but it works for now.

Let's use this object in our original method:

```
public async saveUserDetails(user: UserForStorage) : Promise<void> {
    // Save the data.
}
```

Now, it can be called like this:

```
await saveUserDetails(user);
```

That interface is much clearer and more concise. It abstracts all the details away from us so we can understand what the method is doing at a high level without getting confused by all the noise that many parameters and variables produce.

In cases where your data is part of logically different models or *things*, you can use multiple data objects:

```
await saveUserDetails(user, contactInformation);
```

Each of those data objects has many properties of its own that are now abstracted away.

In real projects, you'll find methods with many more parameters than this! But now you know how to tackle them.

Methods That Never End

Identification

Projects grow over time. New features, behaviors and business rules are added. Apart from this, bugs are fixed and optimizations are made.

Over time, this can lead to really long methods if this is not dealt with.

For example, you might find a method like this in a code base:

```
public async processOrder(orderId: string): Promise<ValidationMessage> {
    const user = await this.getUserFromSession();
    const userId = user.id;
    const userRole = user.role;
```

```
    const userAllowed: boolean = await this.userCanModifyOrder(userId,
userRole);

    if(!userAllowed) {
        return new ValidationMessage("Permission denied.");
    }

    let saveAttempts = 1;
    while (saveAttempts > 3) {

        const order = await this.getOrderById(orderId);
        if (order.isActive()) {
            const status: OrderStatus = order.getStatus();

            if (status == OrderStatus.Pending) {
                // do some more stuff
            } else if (status == OrderStatus.Shipped) {
                // do some more stuff
            } else if (status == OrderStatus.Cancelled) {
                // do some stuff
            } else if (status == OrderStatus.Returned) {
                // do more stuff
            }
        } else {
            const archiveOnDate: Date = await this.
getOrderArchiveOnDate(orderId);
            if (order.getOrderedOnDate() > archiveOnDate) {
                // Do some stuff
            }
        }

        const result: OrderUpdateResult = await this.tryUpdateOrder(order);

        if (result == OrderUpdateResult.Successful) {
            return new ValidationMessage("Order updated successfully.");
        } else if (result == OrderUpdateResult.OrderVersionOutOfSync) {
            return new ValidationMessage("Order is outdated. Try again.");
        } else if(result == OrderUpdateResult.NetworkError) {
```

```
            saveAttempts++;
            // The while loop will try to process the order again.
        }
    }
}
```

Did you get all that?

Well, that's a hard method to glance at and figure out what it's doing. It's too long.

In reality, this method is not that long *compared to what you'll face in real code bases.*

I've seen methods that are more than 5,000 lines of code. I've had colleagues who have worked with methods so long that their IDE couldn't even load the file...

This method is organized fairly *okay*. It's pretty flat (in terms of nesting) and it's using some refactoring techniques we've gone over before (using enums instead of Booleans, failing fast when the user doesn't have permission to change the order, and so on).

Usually, when you find a long method, it's been neglected and exhibits many of the code smells we've gone over.

When Is a Method Too Long?

So, when does a method become too long?

I've heard people give metrics such as *no longer than 10 lines.* I don't think that's helpful.

What I've found to be a helpful and very straightforward guideline is: if a method is longer than the screen/monitor you are looking at it on, then it's probably too long.

That's worked well for me.

The preceding method just barely extends beyond my monitor's height when viewing it in Visual Studio Code. So... let's refactor it!

Give It a Name

The piece of code from the previous chapter is a *doozy*.

One of the main issues with long methods is that there's too much for your brain to process. There's too much going on; too much noise.

The quickest and most effective way to reduce this cognitive overload is by abstracting the main sections or *ideas* in our method into other smaller, more specific, methods.

Usually, we think about methods as a tool for sharing code. But that's not the main purpose of methods. The main purpose is that they help us to abstract parts of our code and give that code a more understandable label.

> **Note**
>
> Methods are not designed primarily as a mechanism to *share code* but as a way to *abstract implementation details.*

I'm going to show you the code example again, but with some added comments around where I think some natural *seams* for creating new methods might be:

```
public async processOrder(orderId: string): Promise<ValidationMessage> {
+    // This section simply checks if a user is allowed
+    // to modify the order.
     const user = await this.getUserFromSession();
     const userId = user.id;
     const userRole = user.role;

     const userAllowed: boolean = await this.userCanModifyOrder(userId,
userRole);

     if(!userAllowed) {
         return new ValidationMessage("Permission denied.");
     }

+    // This loop is just to retry processing the order
+    // whenever there's a network error.
+    // It could be changed into a reusable higher-order function.
     let saveAttempts = 1;
     while (saveAttempts > 3) {

+        // This is where the core logic begins.
         const order = await this.getOrderById(orderId);
         if (order.isActive()) {
             const status: OrderStatus = order.getStatus();

             if (status == OrderStatus.Pending) {
+                // Pending logic.
             } else if (status == OrderStatus.Shipped) {
+                // Shipped logic.
```

```
         } else if (status == OrderStatus.Cancelled) {
+            // Cancelled logic.
         } else if (status == OrderStatus.Returned) {
+            // Returned order logic.
         }
     } else {
+        // Logic to see if order needs to be archived.
         const archiveOnDate: Date = await this.
getOrderArchiveOnDate(orderId);
         if (order.getOrderedOnDate() > archiveOnDate) {
             // Do some stuff
         }
     }

+    // This is where we save the order and deal with the result.
     const result: OrderUpdateResult = await this.tryUpdateOrder(order);

     if (result == OrderUpdateResult.Successful) {
         return new ValidationMessage("Order updated successfully.");
     } else if (result == OrderUpdateResult.OrderVersionOutOfSync) {
         return new ValidationMessage("Order is outdated. Try again.");
     } else if(result == OrderUpdateResult.NetworkError) {
         saveAttempts++;
         // The while loop will try to process the order again.
     }
   }
}
```

Let's take those comments and change a few of the sections into new methods. This should better abstract the details away and let us better name/label each of these sections:

```
const userAllowed: boolean = await this.sessionUserCanModifyOrder();

if(!userAllowed) {
    return new ValidationMessage("User not allowed.");
}

const threeTimes = 3;
return this.retry(threeTimes, () => this.processOrder(orderId));
```

Well, that's much simpler! Let's take a look inside the **processOrder** method (which also has its methods extracted):

```
public async processOrder(orderId: string): Promise<void> {
    const order = await this.getOrderById(this.orderId);
    if (order.isActive()) {
        this.processActiveOrder(order);
    } else {
        this.tryArchivingOrder(order);
    }

    return await tryUpdateOrder(order);
}
```

We can keep going deeper and deeper into these new methods that we've extracted.

Notice that instead of having *one level of methods*, we have *multiple levels of methods*. This is usually what happens–there are multiple levels of logic that end up being extracted.

Keeping each method very short makes our code very readable and easy to understand!

Being Strategic

We're going to continue working with the code we refactored in the previous sections.

By extracting more specialized and targeted methods, we were able to abstract the details down to lower levels and label our logic.

Another cause of long methods that I've seen is when you get sections of code with lengthy logic inside conditionals.

Let's take this one in particular (which has some simulated logic):

```
const status: OrderStatus = order.getStatus();

if (status == OrderStatus.Pending) {
  // Lots of logic.
  // Lots more logic.
  // Lots more logic.
  // Lots more logic.
  // Lots more logic.
  // Lots more logic.
  // Lots more logic.
```

```
} else if (status == OrderStatus.Shipped) {
 // Lots of logic.
 // Lots more logic.
 // Lots more logic.
 // Lots more logic.
 // Lots more logic.
 // Lots more logic.
 // Lots more logic.
} else if (status == OrderStatus.Cancelled) {
 // Lots of logic.
 // Lots more logic.
 // Lots more logic.
 // Lots more logic.
 // Lots more logic.
 // Lots more logic.
 // Lots more logic.
} else if (status == OrderStatus.Returned) {
 // Lots of logic.
 // Lots more logic.
 // Lots more logic.
 // Lots more logic.
 // Lots more logic.
 // Lots more logic.
 // Lots more logic.
}
```

The classic refactoring for whenever you see these lengthy conditionals is the strategy pattern.

Here's one form that we could use:

```
// This works with an enum having numerically backed values.
enum OrderStatus {
 Pending = 0,
 Shipped = 1,
 Cancelled = 2,
 Returned = 3
}

// In our method...
```

```
const strategies: Function[] = [];
strategies[OrderStatus.Pending] = this.processPendingOrder;
strategies[OrderStatus.Shipped] = this.processShippedOrder;
strategies[OrderStatus.Cancelled] = this.processCancelledOrder;
strategies[OrderStatus.Returned] = this.processReturnedOrder;

// Execute the appropriate strategy.
strategies[order.getStatus()]();
```

If we wanted to add any additional branches of logic it would now be much easier to do. This code is compact and it's easy to see what methods are associated with which order statuses.

If, for example, **processPendingOrder** is a complex piece of logic, we don't need to know or deal with it at this level.

Combined with other refactoring techniques, this can go a long way to making your code healthier and easy to understand!

8

Dumping Grounds

Identification

Earlier in my career, I faced a sort of career crisis.

I was part of a team creating a large analytics platform in the automotive industry. The application had the typical *enterprisey* layered architecture you would expect (*Business Layer*, *Data Access Layer*, *Core*, and so on).

You would expect to find business logic – the really important business logic – embedded somewhere inside of the code for these layers. But usually, the really important business rules were coded in stored procedures.

> **Note**
>
> Stored procedures, in case you don't know, are like functions you create inside of a database that use SQL-like syntax to process data, store it, and so on.

I wondered what the purpose of the layers was. They didn't have any code except for passing data to stored procedures or showing data returned by one.

I started to learn more about object-oriented programming (OOP), industry best practices, SOLID, other programming paradigms, application architecture, and so on.

From this career crisis, I discovered that these problems have already been solved! It just takes research, time, and practice to learn and grow skilled in them.

Object-Oriented?

One thing I discovered is that all the projects I've worked on that involved *object-oriented* programming were *not* doing true OOP. Just because you use classes doesn't mean you are doing OOP, especially if you are using stored procedures to encode all your business rules.

The Great Debate

It needs to be brought up... What's better: object-oriented programming or functional programming (FP)?

For starters, most people don't understand what OOP was intended to be in the first place. Similar to how, today, Agile is usually misunderstood (for example, just because you are having daily stand-ups and using story points and kanban, and so on doesn't mean you are doing Agile).

Alan Kay is considered the father of OOP, in a sense. In a certain email (http://userpage.
fu-berlin.de/~ram/pub/pub_jf47ht81Ht/doc_kay_oop_en), he gave some frank
explanations about what OOP was supposed to be.

> **Note**
>
> He said "I thought of objects being like biological cells and/or individual computers
> on a network, only able to communicate with messages (so messaging came at
> the very beginning – it took a while to see how to do messaging in a programming
> language efficiently enough to be useful)...
>
> OOP to me means only messaging, local retention and protection and hiding of
> state-process, and extreme late-binding of all things...
>
> But just to show how stubbornly an idea can hang on, all through the seventies
> and eighties, there were many people who tried to get by with "Remote Procedure
> Call" instead of thinking about objects and messages."

For those familiar with microservices, the actor model, and other advanced
programming paradigms, your Spidey sense is tingling. These are actually more closely
related to true OOP.

So, is FP better than true OOP?

I don't think so. I think they both have their merits. Languages such as TypeScript
embrace both paradigms and allow developers to use the tools and methods that work
best for the given problem!

What you'll usually find are classes that expose all their properties or internal data
members. An HTTP request or database query will fill up all the properties, and then,
perhaps, something else will work on that object's data.

So, instead of what Alan Kay intended to be as little *bundles* that pass messages to
each other (see the preceding box), most developers use objects as mere *data holders*.
Glorified variables, as it were.

What you'll also find in many code bases are very generic classes such as *User*, *Customer*, and *Order*.

Is that bad? Well, *yes*.

Let me ask you a question: Is *User* used in many different unrelated places in your application? For example, is your *User* class used in the billing part of your code, the user profile parts, the shipping parts, and so on?

Most systems do something like that.

What will end up happening is that, because these classes are so generic, *they'll become dumping grounds for code that we don't know where it belongs.*

Instead of taking the time to think about the business need for this new code we've written, often, we feel that it's easier to put it into our generic classes. It's all sharable, right? And we're all about code reuse, right?

Coupling

So... what if I changed the **User** class to conform to some billing logic? What are the chances that I've also broken the shipping feature by changing this class? I don't know, but it's *higher than 0%*.

This **User** class has coupled all your features together. This causes lots of problems.

Ideally, we want our code to be orthogonal (that's just a fancy word that means changing code in one place won't affect other unrelated places).

We want to be able to change the shipping feature, for example, and *not have to test our entire application again*. But if we're sharing our **User** class everywhere, to have confidence that we didn't break stuff, we need to re-test *everything*.

This leads to a fear of changing code. The fear of making our code better. It also leads to a lot of bugs. If you are building out the payment feature for your application, you shouldn't have to think about whether you are breaking the shipping feature at the same time! This causes a huge cognitive load that doesn't need to be there.

Let's continue by looking at a few of my favorite techniques to solve this problem.

Warning Sign

Overall, I find that the idea of segmenting your business features/functions via different physical folders or even entirely different projects altogether is best. I've written about this before (https://dev.to/jamesmh/the-life-changing-and-time-saving-magic-of-feature-focused-code-organization-1708).

But when it comes to our code at a deeper level, we can still tend to design our classes and objects in a way that's still too generic and leads to a lot of coupling.

Anytime I find classes that have simple names such as `User` or `Customer`, an alarm goes off. I'd much rather see classes that are created for a specific context.

For example, if I saw a class named `UserForAuthentication` or `PaymentsCustomer`, then I would be more confident that those classes aren't being thrown around and reused in too many contexts.

Here's a basic technique that might help you get started on analyzing your classes. Take your class name and answer these questions:

1. Is there a subject (user, client, order, and so on)?
2. Is there a context for that subject (shipping, orders, dashboard, and so on)?
3. Is there even perhaps an action being performed on the subject (as we'll see in more detail soon)?

If you cannot answer two of those questions, then I'd say there's a good chance that your class might be doing too much by being too generic.

One of These Things Is Not Like The Others

There's a programming principle we saw earlier in the book called the **Single Responsibility Principle**.

When looking at classes or methods that are doing too much, using the SRP as a guiding light can help us to make code that is easier to maintain, less coupled, and therefore leads to fewer bugs.

Let's look at a generic **User** class that might be similar to code that you've seen before:

```
class User {
    public firstName: string;
    public lastName: string;
    public id: number;
    public jwtToken: string;
    public homeAddress: string;
    public creditCardNo: string;

    public getFullName(): string {
        return this.firstName + " " + this.lastName;
    }

    public decodeJwtToken(): string {
        return decode(this.jwtToken);
    }
}
```

Look familiar?

Given the name of the class, we should start to be suspicious that it's too generic a class...

You Have Mail

You've been tasked with adding a new business requirement. We need users to be able to pay for their products using PayPal.

This **User** class is already used in multiple places, such as the user profile, shipping, and payment features.

All we need to do is add the user's PayPal email address to the user. Right?

Breaking It Up

Usually, you will get new business requirements that require *more* changes to your code than this. But this is a simple example.

If we start changing this **User** class so that it works with the payment feature, then we risk affecting the user profile or the shipping feature (since they use this class too).

What should we do?

The best thing to do here is to *create* a different **User** class that's used *within each specific context*.

Out of this should come classes such as **UserForAuthentication**, **UserProfileUser**, **ShippingUser**, and **PaymentUser**.

Are those models/classes going to contain similar pieces of data that all of them will need? Sure.

Will they also have pieces of data that are only used in one context? Sure. For example, the user's **id** is needed everywhere. But the user's home address is only ever needed for shipping. Why, then, does the payment feature need access to that data? It doesn't.

Here's what these classes might look like:

```
class UserProfileUser {
    public firstName: string;
    public lastName: string;
    public id: number;
    public homeAddress: string;

    public getFullName(): string {
        return this.firstName + " " + this.lastName;
    }
}

class ShippingUser {
    public id: number;
    public homeAddress: string;
}

class UserForAuthentication {
    public id: number;
    public jwtToken: string;

    public decodeJwtToken(): string {
        return decode(this.jwtToken);
    }
}

class PaymentUser {
```

```
    public id: number;
    public creditCardNo: string;
}
```

Keep Separate Things Separate

Notice that the home address is needed by **UserProfileUser** and **ShippingUser**. Is that bad?

We've had it drilled into us so much that duplicating code is a bad thing – so much so that it's that idea that's caused the problems we're talking about right now!

Sometimes, it's better to duplicate code and/or data if they are within different contexts. Again, we want to avoid coupling our features and classes together.

Let me ask you a question: Is it probable that the behavior for the home address within the user's profile will be different than the behavior for it in the shipping feature?

The answer: *yes.*

So, we are talking about two different things. It's the same raw data but not the same business function or concept. **Shipping** needs the home address so that it knows *where to send products.* The user profile needs the home address so the user can *update its values from a UI.*

Not the same thing.

Also, consider that it might also make sense to add an address to the **PaymentUser** class. But should this context share the same address as shipping? Well, is it possible that your shipping address wouldn't be the same address you want to bill to? Sure! This happens all the time!

Using the SRP, we see that these two concepts/responsibilities should be kept separate.

Also, notice that most of our pieces of data are *not* being shared. The JWT, for example, is only needed for authenticating a user. Why would we ever need that piece of data inside our shipping feature's code?

Now, that information is isolated.

Also, any methods that act on that data will also be moved and not inappropriately called by another feature's code.

This was a simple example and, in most cases, it can get a little trickier than we might want. In the end, though, keeping different business concepts separate from each other will make your code easier to understand within a specific context, easier to maintain, and less error-prone!

Speak or Listen

In the previous section, we learned about keeping our objects and methods separate, even when it seems at first glance that they are the same things or concepts.

After further analysis, we found that our code could be de-coupled, isolated, and modularized by paying attention not to *data* but to *behavior* and *business functions*.

This chapter is also about taking this idea of *splitting* our classes into different kinds of responsibilities.

CQRS

CQRS stands for Command Query Responsibility Segregation. It's a pattern that can be helpful when dealing with more complex business logic.

Well, I prefer to use it most of the time anyway, since it makes things much easier to reason about and removes even more coupling from our code.

At a very basic level, though (the level we are going to look at), the core idea is that you should always create different classes that deal with writes and reads.

Read and Write

Usually, when we create classes, they are used in both write and read scenarios. So, for example, a **PaymentUser** class will have methods for modifying its data or applying business rules, and also methods or properties that are used in scenarios where we are displaying data to a user.

You might see a class like this:

```
class PaymentUser {
    public id: number;
    public firstName: string;
    public lastName: string;
    public creditCardNo: string;

    public changeCreditCard(newNumber: string) {
        if(this.validCreditCard(newNumber)) {
            this.creditCardNo = newNumber;
        } else {
            throw 'Invalid credit card number.';
```

```
        }
    }

    public displayName() {
        return this.lastName + ", " + this.firstName;
    }
}
```

Notice that the **changeCreditCard** method is a write method. It changes the state of our object and applies a certain business rule (that only a valid credit card can be used/stored).

However, the **displayName** method is used to show data on a UI.

Here's my question: Why are both of these different concerns in the same place?

These kinds of classes can quickly become confusing. We also tend to start loading them up with tons of display logic or tons of business rules. This makes them hard to understand and reason about.

So, instead, why don't we separate our model/class into *two*?

```
class PaymentUserForDisplay {
    public id: number;
    public firstName: string;
    public lastName: string;
    public creditCardNo: string;

    public displayName() {
        return this.lastName + ", " + this.firstName;
    }
}

class PaymentUserForWrite {
    public id: number;
    public creditCardNo: string;

    public changeCreditCard(newNumber: string) {
        if(this.validCreditCard(newNumber)) {
            this.creditCardNo = newNumber;
        } else {
            throw 'Invalid credit card number.';
        }
    }
}
```

Notice, as in the previous chapter, both models/classes do contain some of the same data (**id**). That's fine. We are dealing with two different contexts and therefore two different business usages or scenarios.

> **Note**
>
> What we currently have with **PaymentUserForWrite** is similar to the concept of aggregates in Domain-Driven Design (https://lostechies. com/jimmybogard/2008/05/21/entities-value-objects-aggregates-and-roots/#aggregates-and-roots).

Next Steps

Creating **PaymentUserForWrite** is a good first step. But the CQRS pattern tells us to take this even further. Imagine that **PaymentUserForWrite** had many other *write* methods that had business logic in them. How could we deal with that complexity?

We would need to look at the intention of the users using our system.

One of the scenarios required is the ability for a user to *update their credit card information*. This specific scenario is currently modeled by the **changeCreditCard** method.

As we know, business rules and logic are often more complex than in this code example, and there are many other business rules for other scenarios that we'll need in our class.

What can we do to simplify things and make it easier to deal with?

Well, we'll take each business scenario and create a class to model that exact scenario! Each of these classes will either be read-only or write-only:

- Commands: These are scenarios that change our system but don't return data to the user to display.

- Queries: Scenarios where we display data to a user so that they can decide on something.

Commands

In the case of *updating a user's credit card information*, we'll create a class to model this:

```
class UpdateUserCreditCardInfoCommand {
    public id: number;
    public creditCardNo: string;

    public handle(newNumber: string) {
        if(this.validCreditCard(newNumber)) {
            this.creditCardNo = newNumber;
        } else {
            throw 'Invalid credit card number.';
        }
    }
}
```

This is a very primitive example. Usually, there would be more to this. But what I want to focus on is the idea of making your classes handle specific business scenarios *and nothing more.*

There's no chance of unintentionally changing this class unless you were *working on this specific business use case.*

Queries

Since we've split our **PaymentUser** into two, we can create specific classes for business scenarios that display data to users.

PaymentUserForDisplay might still be too generic, so in the case of a user profile UI, we might create a specific query class to fetch and display this data:

```
class UserProfileQuery {
    public id: number;
    public firstName: string;
    public lastName: string;
    public creditCardNo: string;

    public handle(forUserId: number) {
        const userData: UserProfileData = await this.fetch(forUserId);
        // Assign fields
    }
}
```

Usually, you want your query class to return a different type of view model:

```
class UserProfileView {
    public id: number;
    public firstName: string;
    public lastName: string;
    public creditCardNo: string;
}

class UserProfileQuery {
    public async handle(forUserId: number): UserProfileView {
        const view: UserProfileView = await this.fetch(forUserId);
        return view;
    }
}
```

Conclusion

We started with a class that, in theory, was getting out of hand, with both read and write behaviors.

By splitting this class even more into read and write appropriate models, each specific class is much easier to deal with. They are not coupled to each other, and they allow different UI scenarios the ability to display different data, if needed, without bloating the same class (since we aren't sharing a class throughout different scenarios).

A Word of Caution

Just to make it clear, this isn't refactoring that you necessarily ought to always implement. It depends on your project needs and the complexity of your business rules and logic.

That being said, I've found this pattern more helpful than not. Keeping different concerns separated from each other, in the end, leads to code that is much more maintainable, easier to read, and easier to extend.

For a deeper dive into CQRS, I'd recommend the following:

- A virtual meeting on the topic (https://www.youtube.com/watch?v=5e7lhY2q8WQ)

- An article by Jimmy Bogard (https://lostechies.com/jimmybogard/2015/05/05/cqrs-with-mediatr-and-automapper/)

- Another article by Jimmy (https://lostechies.com/jimmybogard/2012/08/22/busting-some-cqrs-myths/)

9

Messy Object Creation

Identification

At times, even after we have tried to make the various parts of our code as small and modular as we can, there are cases when we still have to create some complex objects.

In a hypothetical software project that's being used in the airline industry, you might come across code like this:

```
const plane = new Airplane();

plane.type = PlaneType.Passenger;
plane.engine = new PassengerPlaneEngine();

plane.hasFirstClass = true;
plane.hasBathroom = false;
```

```
plane.numberOfSeats = 100;
// etc.
```

As a smaller sample of a larger piece of code, this might not look *too bad*.

What you'll probably find is that this kind of code will be copied and pasted into other places. So, whenever we need to create a passenger plane that has 100 seats, someone might decide to copy and paste this code *just this one time*.

Especially in teams with less experienced developers (even developers who've been in the industry for years can be inexperienced!), you'll often find poor practices such as copying and pasting, creating objects and then mucking with their internal properties, and so on, being used as quick shortcuts.

Over time, though, creating code that allows the caller to reach into these objects and set all the parameters of an object come back to haunt you. Yes, it seems *flexible*, but it's not maintainable. These kinds of classes are notoriously hard to test too.

When they've been copied and pasted, fixing bugs becomes hard because there's no central place to fix where all passenger planes are being created (for example).

In the next couple of chapters, we'll look at some ways to create objects that allow your code to stay flexible yet become maintainable and testable.

Factory Functions

Sticking with our airplane example, we've got:

```
const plane = new Airplane();

plane.type = PlaneType.Passenger;
plane.engine = new PassengerPlaneEngine();

plane.hasFirstClass = true;
plane.hasBathroom = false;
plane.numberOfSeats = 100;
// etc.
```

In another place within this airline application, you need to write some code that does the same thing except makes the **numberOfSeats** variable a different value:

```
plane.numberOfSeats = 50;
```

Should we copy and paste all the code that creates a new airplane? Of course not!

Instead, we can create targeted functions that will deal with creating the airplane for us. These are called *Factory Functions*.

This will allow us to easily create a new airplane whenever we want and also gain the benefits of being able to configure how that plane is built:

```
const createPassengerPlane = (numberOfSeats: number): Airplane => {
    const plane = new Airplane();

    plane.type = PlaneType.Passenger;
    plane.engine = new PassengerPlaneEngine();

    plane.hasFirstClass = true;
    plane.hasBathroom = false;
    plane.numberOfSeats = numberOfSeats;

    return plane;
}
```

> **Note**
>
> You can export this as part of a JavaScript/TypeScript module.

Now, to create a new passenger airplane, all you need to do is:

```
const plane1 = createPassengerPlane(100);
const plane2 = createPassengerPlane(50);
```

That's much cleaner, and we can reuse this function throughout our app!

Functions versus Static Methods

Depending on the context and your preference, you might want to make factory functions static methods that live inside an **AirplaneFactory** class:

```
class AirplaneFactory {
    public static createPassengerPlane = (numberOfSeats: number): Airplane => {
        const plane = new Airplane();

        plane.type = PlaneType.Passenger;
```

```
        plane.engine = new PassengerPlaneEngine();

        plane.hasFirstClass = true;
        plane.hasBathroom = false;
        plane.numberOfSeats = numberOfSeats;

        return plane;
    }
}
```

This would be used like so:

```
const plane3 = AirplaneFactory.createPassengerPlane(100);
```

Especially in languages such as Java and C#, this is used as a way to organize these factory functions in one cohesive place. These languages don't allow programmers to define functions outside of classes.

However, in TypeScript, you can. And you can expose/export them via a module. Therefore, in TypeScript, doing this in a module is preferred. But it's always good to know how this might be done in more class-oriented languages.

Combining Refactoring Techniques

Imagine a business came to you and gave you some requirements for a new feature. This will require the ability to be able to create many different kinds of planes while being able to define all their possible parameters, such as the number of seats, whether there is a bathroom, and so on.

In the previous section, we created a factory function. Given these new requirements, our function might look like this now:

```
const createPlane =
    (
        type: PlaneType,
        engine: IPlaneEngine,
        hasFirstClass: boolean,
        hasBathroom: boolean,
        numberOfSeats: number
    ): Airplane => {

    const plane = new Airplane();
```

```
    plane.type = type;
    plane.engine = engine;
    plane.hasFirstClass = hasFirstClass;
    plane.hasBathroom = hasBathroom;
    plane.numberOfSeats = numberOfSeats;

    return plane;
}
```

When used, it might look like this:

```
const plane = createPlane(
    PlaneType.Passenger,
    new PassengerPlaneEngine(),
    true,
    true,
    100
);
```

There's an entire section about dealing with methods that have many parameters in this book. What would happen if we extracted a data object and used it in this context?

```
class PlaneCreationOptions {
    public type: PlaneType;
    public engine: IPlaneEngine;
    public hasFirstClass: boolean;
    public hasBathroom: boolean;
    public numberOfSeats: number;
}

// The only param now is the data object we created.
const createPlane = (options: PlaneCreationOptions): Airplane => {
    const plane = new Airplane();

    plane.type = options.type;
    plane.engine = options.engine;
    plane.hasFirstClass = options.hasFirstClass;
    plane.hasBathroom = options.hasBathroom;
    plane.numberOfSeats = options.numberOfSeats;

    return plane;
}
```

It would look something like this in use:

```
const options = new PlaneCreationOptions();
options.type = PlaneType.Passenger;
options.engine = new PassengerPlaneEngine();
options.hasFirstClass = true;
options.hasBathroom = true;
options.numberOfSeats = 100;

const plane = createPlane(options);
```

This does seem much cleaner and clearer regarding what specific properties of the plane are being configured.

Complexity Remains...

This looks great. But there's a problem.

When we decided to create a factory function in the previous section, that method was really simple and straightforward to call:

```
const plane1 = createPassengerPlane(100);
const plane2 = createPassengerPlane(50);
```

Now, though, we introduced a bit more complexity when assigning these properties. Trying to replicate the code in the preceding snippet using the data object we created would look like this:

```
const options = new PlaneCreationOptions();
options.type = PlaneType.Passenger;
options.engine = new PassengerPlaneEngine();
options.hasFirstClass = true;
options.hasBathroom = true;
options.numberOfSeats = 100;

const plane1 = createPlane(options);

options.numberOfSeats = 50;

const plane2 = createPlane(options);
```

First off, we are reusing the same **PlaneCreationOptions** object for both plane creations. This might not be the best idea in terms of maintainable and easy-to-read code. It would be better to have two separate **options** objects to keep each piece of creation logic isolated. But that would also mean a lot more code...

That being said, it does seem like there is a lot of code that – somehow – could be simplified.

Building It

We've created a special function to create planes. But now we've just moved the complexity into our **data** object.

What if we could find a way to still have the flexibility of being able to specify any of the different parameters available when creating a plane, yet still have a simple way to create a plane in scenarios where we only need to set one or two parameters?

```
const fullyLoadedPassengerOptions = () => {
    const options = new PlaneCreationOptions();
    options.type = PlaneType.Passenger;
    options.engine = new PassengerPlaneEngine();
    options.hasFirstClass = true;
    options.hasBathroom = true;
    options.numberOfSeats = 100;
    return options;
}

const bareBonesPassengerOptions = () => {
    const options = new PlaneCreationOptions();
    options.type = PlaneType.Passenger;
    options.engine = new PassengerPlaneEngine();
    options.hasFirstClass = false;
    options.hasBathroom = false;
    options.numberOfSeats = 10;
    return options;
}
```

We've created some factory methods for our plane creation data object! Now we can use it like this:

```
const plane1 = createPlane(fullyLoadedPassengerOptions());

const bareBones = bareBonesPassengerOptions();
bareBones.numberOfSeats = 50;
const plane2 = createPlane(bareBones);
```

Awesome!

The Builder Pattern

This is a take on the Builder Pattern. In class-based languages such as Java, this involves creating some classes and can get a little tricky.

But in TypeScript, we can just create autonomous *builder* functions. That's the great thing about TypeScript: you have tons of flexibility in how you want to do things.

One Last Improvement

There is one more improvement we can make.

Usually, when using the builder pattern, these *options* or *builder* classes are often easier to use with a fluent programming style. A fluent programming style is when you can chain method calls from an object (like jQuery).

Let's modify our **PlaneCreationOptions** class:

```
class PlaneCreationOptions {
    // All the public properties...

    public withSeats(numberOfSeats: number) {
        this.numberOfSeats = numberOfSeats;
        return this;
    }

    // Etc.
}
```

Now, our code will look like this in use:

```
const plane1 = createPlane(fullyLoadedPassengerOptions());
const plane2 = createPlane(bareBonesPassengerOptions().withSeats(50));
```

That's much simpler, easier to read, and would be super easy to test!

10
Conclusion

This Is Just The Beginning!

Throughout this book, you've learned all about refactoring: what it is, why it's important, and how to do it!

But this book is just the beginning. There are still *tons* of code smells that haven't been addressed in this book. There are many more techniques, even for the issues covered in this book.

In addition to code health, there are many more areas where, as a professional software developer, you need to understand the warning signs of disease:

- Application architecture
- Business processes

- Peer relationships

- Product market fit

- User impact

Ideally, as a professional business problem-solver (that's what you are, after all!), you will grow in your craft, impact, and career. As you grow, you'll find yourself having more influence and impact in terms of helping your teammates, managers, users, products, and organizations improve as a whole.

It's not all about code but solving tough and important business problems.

But those are topics for another day!

There are many excellent resources out there for further reading on this subject. This book has set you off on a journey of refactoring, and you are encouraged to go and learn as much as you can. Other than further reading around the subject, the best way to discover more is through practice. Go ahead and start analyzing the code you're working with to see where and how it can be improved. Good luck!

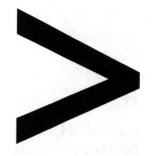

Index

About

All major keywords used in this book are captured alphabetically in this section. Each one is accompanied by the page number of where they appear.

V

W